When the Teacher Isn't Looking

AND OTHER FUNNY SCHOOL POEMS

Kenn Nesbitt
Illustrated by Mike Gordon

𝓂 Meadowbrook Press

Distributed by Simon & Schuster
New York

Library of Congress Cataloging-in-Publication Data

Nesbitt, Kenn.
 When the teacher isn't looking : and other funny school poems / written by Kenn Nesbitt ;
illustrated by Mike Gordon.
    p. cm.
Summary: "A collection of humorous poems about the ups and downs of going to
school"—Provided by publisher.
ISBN 0-88166-489-8 (Meadowbrook Press), ISBN 0-684-03128-0 (Simon & Schuster)
1. Schools—Juvenile poetry. 2. Education—Juvenile poetry. 3. Children's poetry,
American. 4. Humorous poetry, American. I. Gordon, Mike. II. Title.
PS3614.E47W47 2005
811'.54—dc22
                              2004024948

Editorial Director: Christine Zuchora-Walske
Editor: Bruce Lansky
Coordinating Editor and Copyeditor: Angela Wiechmann
Production Manager: Paul Woods
Graphic Design Manager: Tamara Peterson
Illustrations and Cover Art: Mike Gordon

Published by Meadowbrook Press, 5451 Smetana Drive, Minnetonka, Minnesota 55343

www.meadowbrookpress.com

BOOK TRADE DISTRIBUTION by Simon and Schuster, a division of Simon and Schuster,
Inc., 1230 Avenue of the Americas, New York, New York 10020

10 09 08 07 06 05   10 9 8 7 6 5 4 3 2 1

Printed in the United States of America

Dedication

To J. J., Ricky, and Jo

Acknowledgments

Thank you, Ann, for your encouragement and support, which made this book possible. Thank you, Max and Madison, for laughing at my poems, even when you didn't get the jokes. Thank you, Eric Herman, for the spatula. Thank you, Bruce Lansky, for believing in me and for all you do to bring funny poetry to kids everywhere. Thank you, Angie Wiechmann, for putting all my commas in the right places. And a special thank-you to all the schoolteachers who do the most important work of all—sharing poems with your students, creating a whole new generation of poetry lovers.

Many thanks to the following teachers and their students who tested poems for this collection:

Diane Clapp, Lincoln Elementary, Faribault, MN
Connie Cooper, Lincoln Elementary, Faribault, MN
Marianne Gately, McCarthy Elementary, Framingham, MA
Sandra Kane, Lincoln Elementary, Faribault, MN
Kathy Kenney-Marshall, McCarthy Elementary, Framingham, MA
Carolyn Larsen, Rum River Elementary, Andover, MN
Carol Larson, Rum River Elementary, Andover, MN
Carmen Markgren, East Elementary, New Richmond, WI
Jenny Myer, East Elementary, New Richmond, WI
Mary Niermann, Lincoln Elementary, Faribault, MN
Jim Parr, McCarthy Elementary, Framingham, MA
John Pundsack, East Elementary, New Richmond, WI
Ruth Refsnider, East Elementary, New Richmond, WI
Cathy Rodrigue, Deer Creek Elementary, Crowley, TX
Connie Roetzer, East Elementary, New Richmond, WI
Andrea Rutkowski, Miscoe Hill Elementary, Mendon, MA
Beverly Semanko, Rum River Elementary, Andover, MN
Maria Smith, Deer Creek Elementary, Crowley, TX
Carleen Tjader, East Elementary, New Richmond, WI
Margie Thell Weiss, East Elementary, New Richmond, WI
Julie White, East Elementary, New Richmond, WI

Contents

I Can't Wait for Summer

I can't wait for summer, when school days are done,
to spend the days playing outside in the sun.
I won't have to study. No homework, no tests.
Just afternoons spent on adventures and quests.

Instead of mathematics and writing reports,
I'll go to the park and play summertime sports.
Instead of assignments, report cards, and grades,
I'll get to play baseball and watch the parades.

I'll swing on the playground. I'll swim in the pool
instead of just practicing lessons in school.
The second the school year is finally done
I'll spend every minute with friends having fun.

I hardly can wait for the end of the year.
I'm counting the days until summer is here.
It's hard to be patient. It's hard to be cool.
It's hard to believe it's the first day of school.

Getting Dressed for School

I must have been too sleepy
getting dressed for school today.
I tried to tuck my shirt in,
but I couldn't make it stay.

I also couldn't tie my shoes.
I fumbled with the laces.
I snagged my scarf, and now some yarn
is dangling from my braces.

My socks are different colors,
and my pants are inside out.
My sweater from the hamper left me
smelling like a trout.

I thought I put a hat on
to control my crazy hair.
The hat turned out to be a pair
of purple underwear.

I spilled my breakfast on my clothes
and headed into school.
My friends, of course, were all impressed.
I'd never looked so cool.

Running Late

I overslept. I'm running late.
My mom is making such a fuss.
If I so much as hesitate
I probably will miss the bus.

I grab my socks and underwear
and quickly pull on all my clothes.
I haven't time to comb my hair
or brush my teeth or blow my nose.

I wolf my breakfast, kiss my mom,
and barrel madly out the door.
I'm feeling anything but calm.
I've never been this late before.

I run like crazy down the street.
I check my watch. It's almost eight.
I wish I'd had some more to eat,
but, man, I simply can't be late.

I barely make it there in time.
To miss the bus would not be cool.
I wouldn't mind except that I'm
the guy who drives the kids to school.

Last Night's Nightmares

Some aliens from outer space
came down in UFOs.
They kidnapped me and shoved
a slimy brain probe up my nose.

A horde of screaming monkeys
chased me halfway to Japan,
and Transylvanian vampire bats
attacked me as I ran.

Demented ogres tackled me
and tied me in a knot,
and wicked witches cackled
as they cooked me in a pot.

A starving three-eyed dinosaur
then drowned me in his drool.
But scarier than all of these,
I dreamed I was in school.

I Wake Today

I wake today,
get out of bed,
then stretch and yawn
and scratch my head.

I find my clothes.
I pull them on.
I wonder where
my homework's gone.

I grab a breakfast
bar for fuel,
and hoist my pack
and head to school.

8

When I arrive
I'm truly shocked.
The lights are off.
The door is locked.

I check my watch.
It's me, not them.
I woke too soon.
It's 4:00 A.M.

9

Bored

As I'm sitting in the classroom
with a blank look on my face,
I am staring out the window
at the emptiness of space.

While the teacher drones, explaining
how to multiply a fraction,
my mind is rolling slowly
to a state of numb inaction.

Now my eyes are growing heavy
and my head begins to fall,
as I drift away to slumberland
against the classroom wall.

I'm awakened by the teacher
as she loudly clears her throat.
It appears while I was napping
all the students took a vote.

I got way more votes than anyone,
and this is my reward:
All my classmates have elected me
the chairman of the bored.

Sharpen, Sharpen, Sharpen

Sharpen, sharpen, sharpen.
I crank the handle fast.
Sharpen, sharpen, sharpen.
Until it's sharp at last.

Scribble, scribble, scribble.
Hey wait! It still won't write.
Sharpen, sharpen, sharpen.
I crank with all my might.

Sharpen, sharpen, sharpen.
It must be done, I guess.
Scribble, scribble, dribble.
Oh goodness, what a mess!

Darn it, darn it, darn it.
I guess I'll start again.
Teacher! Teacher! Teacher!
I need another pen.

12

Ancient Romans, Ancient Greeks

Ancient Romans, ancient Greeks
carved for days or often weeks,
working fingers to the bone,
writing words in blocks of stone.

Just imagine all the yelling
if a Greek messed up her spelling.
Other Greeks, I'm sure, would chase her.
I'm so glad for my eraser.

Our Mother's at a Meeting

Our mother's at a meeting
for some big, important deal
and couldn't be at home tonight
to cook the evening meal.

She left some short instructions
that my sister was to follow.
Instead my sister cooked up things
impossible to swallow.

Like Brussels sprouts in vinegar
and jellybeans in mustard,
an onion-pickle pudding
and a lemon-radish custard.

14

She burned a stick of butter
till the house was filled with smoke,
then fried a pound of pepper
with a half an artichoke.

She put a whole banana
in the blender with a steak,
then mixed it up with tuna fish
and baked it in a cake.

She stirred some chocolate ice cream
with garbanzo beans and bacon.
A single bite was all it took
to leave me feeling shaken.

We should have ordered pizza,
but we didn't know, alas,
my sister is the only kid
who flunked her cooking class.

15

Lost and Found

I have to go to Lost and Found.
I need to have a look around.
I lost my pencil and my pen.
I lost my binder once again.

I lost my scarf, my coat, my hat,
my baseball glove and ball and bat.
I lost my lunch. I lost a shoe,
my wallet, and my money, too.

Today I lost a tooth in class.
I lost my marbles in the grass.
I lost a game of tic-tac-toe.
I lost my head a while ago.

I may have lost my sense of smell
and lost my place in line as well.
I lost my patience, lost my cool.
I lost these things—and more—at school.

I hope I find them in the mound
of missing stuff at Lost and Found.
But most of all, I hope to find
my brain because I've lost my mind.

Brandon Branson's Backpack

Brandon Branson's backpack
is unusually large.
He drags it into school
the way a tugboat drags a barge.

The main compartment holds
about a hundred hardback books.
The outside has a zillion
little pockets, straps, and hooks.

It holds his new harmonica
plus three or four kazoos,
his binder and his lunchbox
and an extra pair of shoes.

A CD player, headphones,
and a TV with remote,
a telephone, computer,
and his winter hat and coat.

His skateboard and his scooter
have their own equipment rack.
It even has a space to park
his bicycle in back.

A teacher found it in the hall
today at 9:15.
She looked around for Brandon,
who was nowhere to be seen.

She got some other teachers,
who considered it and frowned,
then groaned and moaned and pulled
and dragged it off to Lost and Found.

They struggled through the doorway
feeling out of breath and strained,
and all of them were curious
to see what it contained.

They cautiously unzipped it,
and they pulled it open wide,
and there was Brandon Branson
napping happily inside.

17

Sick Day

I'm feeling sick and getting worse.
I think I'd better see the nurse.
I'm sure I should go home today.
It could be fatal if I stay.
I'm nauseated, nearly ill.
I have a fever and a chill.
I have a cold. I have the flu.
I'm turning green and pink and blue.
I have the sweats. I have the shakes,
a stuffy nose, and bellyaches.
My knees are weak. My vision's blurred.
My throat is sore. My voice is slurred.
I'm strewn with head lice, ticks, and mites.
I'm covered in mosquito bites.
I have a cough, a creak, a croak,
a reddish rash from poison oak,
a feeble head, a weakened heart.
I may just faint or fall apart.
I sprained my ankle, stubbed my toes,
and soon I'll start to decompose.
And one more thing I have today
that makes me have to go away.
It's just as bad as all the rest:
I also have a science test.

Alex's Allergy

Alex had an allergy
that no one could explain.
It made him wheeze and cough and sneeze
and moan and groan in pain.

A single slight exposure,
and he'd start to squawk and squeal.
A second time ensured
that he'd be barking like a seal.

He'd salivate and slobber
as his nose began to twitch.
He'd squirm and say his body felt
like one gigantic itch.

At last they found the cause,
which Alex thought was pretty cool.
So now he stays at home;
he is allergic to his school.

Jessica Jean

We planted some beans in our garden in class,
along with some peppers and pumpkins and grass.
We planted them neatly in straight little rows.
But Jessica Jean stuck her bean up her nose.

She did it discreetly, not making a peep.
She pushed with her pinky and poked it in deep,
then kept it a secret, so no one would know.
But, meanwhile, her bean was beginning to grow.

It popped out a leaf on the tiniest stalk.
It grew and unfolded and caused her to squawk,
then rapidly blossomed, becoming a vine,
while Jessica Jean was beginning to whine.

It quickly expanded to cover her lips.
It grew on her shoulders, her elbows, and hips.
It bloomed on her body and covered her clothes,
completely encasing her down to her toes.

It looped on her ankles, engulfing her feet,
cocooning her knees, and obscuring her seat,
concealing her up past the top of her chest,
her arms and her hands and then all of the rest.

And that was the last that has ever been seen
or heard of the student named Jessica Jean.
So always remember to plant them in rows,
and never, *don't ever*, put beans in your nose.

21

"You won't begin to bleat or bawl.
I doubt that it will hurt at all.
I don't expect to see it bruise
or swell your arm and start to ooze.

"There's little chance of bellyaches
or fevers, chills, or sudden shakes.
It's not supposed to cause a cough.
Your arm will likely not fall off.

"I'm guessing that there won't be lots
of itchy red and purple spots.
Convulsions, too, are fairly rare.
I think you'll get to keep your hair.

"In fact, the chance is nearly nil
that you'll become intensely ill
or grow a ghastly greenish hue
or turn into a kangaroo.

"It's nearly certain that you'll not
become a fish or flowerpot.
I'm quite convinced it's fair to say
you won't turn into mush today.

Samantha Cinderella Scott

Samantha Cinderella Scott
was told she'd have to have a shot.
The doctor said, "You're somewhat sick;
I think a shot should do the trick."

He said, "You shouldn't feel a thing,
except perhaps a tiny sting,
a painless prick, a poke, a pinch.
It shouldn't even make you flinch.

"But if you start to shake and cough
or if your head should tumble off,
if you become a moose or mule,
you'll get a day away from school."

Samantha Cinderella Scott
took just a moment, deep in thought,
then yawned the slightest little yawn
and told the doctor, "Bring it on!"

Amanda Ate an Orange

Amanda ate an orange
and an olive and a peach.
Since then her teacher always keeps
the crayons out of reach.

23

Patricia Brought Her Parakeet

Patricia brought her parakeet.
It pecked at Patrick's puppy.
Samantha's salamander swiftly
gobbled Gracie's guppy.

Savannah's snapping turtle
snapped the nose of Franklin's frog.
I'd say Fernando's ferret
went berserk on Daniel's dog.

Poor Jordan found his gerbil
being chased by Katelyn's cat,
and everyone was panicking
'cause Ryan brought his rat.

The teacher screamed and fainted,
and she fell right off her stool.
I guess I shouldn't bring
my pet tarantula to school.

She soon enough recovered,
but you should have heard her yell.
It looks like that's the last time
we'll bring pets for show-and-tell.

Betsy Burped the ABCs

Betsy burped the ABCs,
and Thomas popped his toes.
Andrew sang "Amazing Grace"
with hot dogs in his nose.

Michael dropped the microphone.
It bounced and banged a beat.
Caroline confirmed how many
oysters she could eat.

Jacob juggled seven eggs
and dropped them on his head.
Peg performed a poem
with the hiccups as she read.

Clapping, whooping, shouting,
we screamed, "Encore!" and "Bravo!"
Truly, that was one amazing
student talent show.

Chelsea Had Some Chocolate Milk

Chelsea had some chocolate milk
but spilled it on her shirt.
Jackson got his jacket ripped
while rolling in the dirt.

Emily and Isabella
must have had a fight.
Alexander looks as if
he stayed awake all night.

Abigail is absent,
as are Ryan, Ross, and Ruth.
Max is in pajamas,
and Mackenzie lost a tooth.

Brandon broke his glasses.
Sarah's sweater doesn't fit.
Jacob has a bloody nose,
and Zoe has a zit.

We should all be crabby,
but we're smiling anyway.
Our moms and dads are gonna scream—
today is picture day!

I'm Practicing Telepathy

I'm practicing telepathy.
I'm learning ESP.
I'm getting mental images
like pictures on TV.

I thought I'd pick your brain a bit.
I thought I'd read your mind
to get the answers to this test,
but now I'm in a bind.

I probed your thoughts and consciousness,
and now I guarantee,
we both are gonna flunk
because you're copying from me.

Everyone's from Somewhere Else

Phoenix came from Dallas.
Dallas came from Austin.
Austin came from Lowell.
Lowell came from Boston.

Carolina came from Georgia.
Georgia's from Savannah.
Savannah came from Jackson.
Jackson's from Montana.

Virginia came from Maryland.
Mary's from Dakota.
Dakota's from Saint Paul.
And Paul's from Minnesota.

Madison is from Cheyenne.
Cheyenne is from Nebraska.
I wonder where the teacher's from?
I think maybe Alaska.

29

Our Teacher's Multitalented

Our teacher's multitalented.
He plays guitar and sings.
He paints impressive pictures
and can juggle twenty rings.

He dances like an expert;
he can mambo, tap, and waltz.
He's also quite a gymnast,
doing airborne somersaults.

He's something of a swimmer.
He's a champion at chess.
It's difficult to find a skill
that he does not possess.

He speaks a dozen languages.
He's great at racing cars.
He's masterful at fighting bulls
and studying the stars.

He's good at climbing mountains.
He can wrestle with a bear.
The only thing we wish he'd learn
is how to comb his hair.

When the Teacher Isn't Looking

When the teacher's back is turned,
we never scream and shout.
Never do we drop our books
and try to freak her out.

No one throws a pencil
at the ceiling of the class.
No one tries to hit the fire alarm
and break the glass.

We don't cough in unison
and loudly clear our throats.
No one's shooting paper wads
or passing little notes.

She must think we're so polite.
We never make a peep.
Really, though, it's just because
we all go right to sleep.

32

Falling Asleep in Class

I fell asleep in class today,
as I was awfully bored.
I laid my head upon my desk
and closed my eyes and snored.

I woke to find a piece of paper
sticking to my face.
I'd slobbered on my textbooks,
and my hair was a disgrace.

My clothes were badly rumpled,
and my eyes were glazed and red.
My binder left a three-ring
indentation in my head.

I slept through class, and probably
I would have slept some more,
except my students woke me
as they headed out the door.

Good Morning, Dear Students

"Good morning, dear students," the principal said.
"Please put down your pencils and go back to bed.
Today we will spend the day playing outside,
then take the whole school on a carnival ride.

"We'll learn to eat candy while watching TV,
then listen to records and swing from a tree.
We'll also be learning to draw on the walls,
to scream in the classrooms and run in the halls.

"So bring in your skateboard, your scooter, your bike.
It's time to be different and do what you like.
The teachers are going to give you a rest.
You don't have to study. There won't be a test.

"And if you'd prefer, for a bit of a change,
feel free to go wild and act really strange.
Go put on a clown suit and dye your hair green,
and copy your face on the Xerox machine.

"Tomorrow it's back to the regular grind.
Today, just go crazy. We really don't mind.
So tear up your homework. We'll give you an A.
Oh wait. I'm just kidding. It's April Fools' Day."

35

Good Morning, Mrs. Hamster

The teacher performed an experiment
she probably shouldn't have tried.
Some chemicals flashed and exploded.
She ended up frazzled and fried.

Her eyebrows were sizzling and smoking.
Her clothing was covered with soot.
She looked like a cartoon coyote
whose cannon had just gone kaput.

But something astonishing happened
as soon as her test went awry.
The teacher was caught by the shock wave,
and so was her hamster nearby.

The universe inside the blast zone
was literally rearranged,
affecting the teacher and hamster,
and somehow their brains were exchanged.

The hamster climbed up near the blackboard
and handed out homework galore.
The teacher, by contrast, was squeaking
and crawling around on the floor.

The principal quickly came running
the instant he learned of the news.
The hamster said, "Welcome. Please join us."
Our teacher was sniffing his shoes.

I'm sorry to say our poor teacher
now sits in a cage eating grass.
The principal made her our pet,
and the hamster's in charge of the class.

Ants in the Lunchroom

Appearing this morning at quarter past nine,
they entered our lunchroom and mustered a line.
They seemed to be dancing or whistling a tune,
then ran out the door with a fork and a spoon.

They quickly came back for a knife and a plate,
not bothered at all by the size or the weight.
They grabbed all the glasses and cups they could find.
They bagged every bowl, leaving nothing behind.

They worked through the morning, till midafternoon,
and carried off every last saucer and spoon.
They searched every shelf, and they emptied each drawer,
then pilfered the platters and dashed out the door.

They put on a truly impressive display.
They swiped all the dishes and scurried away.
It's hard to believe, but those ants were so shrewd:
They knew not to eat cafeteria food.

Alphabetical Order

Here at school our seats are
alphabetically assigned.
As and Bs are right up front
while Zs are way behind.

Aaron sits up front in class.
Zack is in the back.
Aaron's always first in line.
The last is always Zack.

Zack, in fact, is always last
for every little thing.
Last for snack and last to leave
and last one on the swing.

You'd think it's bad, but you should see
the sparkle in his eyes
when the cafeteria
serves Mystery Meat Surprise.

The Drinking Fountain

The drinking fountain squirted me.
It shot right up my nose.
It felt as if I'd stuck my nostril
on the garden hose.

It squirted water in my eye
and also in my ear.
I'm having trouble seeing,
and it's awfully hard to hear.

The water squirted east and west.
It squirted north and south.
Upon my shirt, my pants, my hair—
but nothing in my mouth.

I'm sure that soon they'll fix it,
but until then, let me think...
Just whom can I convince that they
should come and have a drink?

Lunchbox Love Note

Inside my lunch
to my surprise
a perfect heart-shaped
love note lies.

The outside says,
"Will you be mine?"
and, "Will you be
my valentine?"

I take it out
and wonder who
would want to tell me
"I love you."

Perhaps a girl
who's much too shy
to hand it to me
eye to eye.

Or maybe it
was sweetly penned
in private by
a secret friend

Who found my lunchbox
sitting by
and slid the note in
on the sly.

Oh, I'd be thrilled
if it were Jo,
the cute one in
the second row.

Or could it be
from Jennifer?
Has she found out
I'm sweet on her?

My mind's abuzz,
my shoulders tense.
I need no more
of this suspense.

My stomach lurching
in my throat,
I open up
my little note.

Then *wham!* as if
it were a bomb,
inside it reads,
"I love you—Mom."

Food Fight

We'd never seen the teachers
in a state of such distress.
The principal was yelling
that the lunchroom was a mess.

It started off so innocent
when someone threw a bun,
but all the other kids decided
they should join the fun.

It instantly turned into
an enormous lunchroom feud,
as students started hurling
all their halfway-eaten food.

A glob went whizzing through the air,
impacting on the wall.
Another chunk went sailing out
the doorway to the hall.

The food was splattered everywhere—
the ceilings, walls, and doors.
A sloppy, gloppy mess was on
the tables and the floors.

And so our good custodian
ran out to grab his mop.
It took him half the afternoon
to clean up all the slop.

The teachers even used some words
we're not supposed to mention.
And that's how all the kids and teachers
wound up in detention.

45

I'm Getting Sick of Peanut Butter

I look inside my lunchbox,
and, oh, what do I see?
A peanut butter sandwich
staring glumly back at me.

I know I had one yesterday,
and, yes, the day before.
In fact, that's all I've eaten
for at least a month or more.

I'm sure tomorrow afternoon
the outlook's just as bleak.
I'll bet I'm having peanut butter
every day this week.

I'm getting sick of peanut butter
sandwiches for lunch.
Why can't I have baloney
or potato chips to munch?

I wish I had lasagna
or a piece of pumpkin pie.
Another day of peanut butter
might just make me cry.

But still this awful sandwich
is in every lunch I take.
You see, it is the only thing
my mom knows how to make.

48

Here lies the body of
Izzy Dunn-Eaton.
It's hard to believe
what he tried.
He tasted the school
cafeteria food,
and Izzy Dunn-Eaton
done died.

Snow Day

"Snow day!"
Fred said.
"All play.
Let's sled!

"No school!
Just snow.
Way cool.
Let's go!"

Fred ran
in shed.
Had plan.
Got sled.

"Go slow,"
Mom said.
"I know,"
said Fred.

50

Up hill
went Fred.
Down hill
Fred sped.

Sled streaked
on past.
Mom shrieked,
"Too fast!"

Snow blew.
"Can't see!"
Fred flew.
Hit tree.

Sled bent.
Fred's head
got dent.
Poor Fred.

He cried.
Now plays
inside
snow days.

51

Jim Sox

He's "Mr. Athletic,"
the coolest of jocks,
the school's fastest runner:
His name is Jim Sox.

He's fearsome at football,
terrific at tennis.
At baseball and basketball
Jim is a menace.

He's always the winner.
There isn't a sport
where Jim doesn't rule
as the king of the court.

He's equally blessed
on the field and the rink,
but all of that exercise
gives him a stink.

And so in our schoolyard
the greatest of knocks
is telling a person,
"You smell like Jim Sox."

What the Teachers Saw at Recess

Mr. D. saw Esau seesaw.
That's what Mr. D. said he saw.
Mrs. C. saw Mr. D. see
Esau seesaw. That's what she saw.

We saw Esau see C. see D.
He saw C. saw D. saw Esau.
Mr. E. was out to sea, so
it's a mystery what he saw.

55

The Dragon on the Playground

There's a dragon on the playground
who descended from the skies.
He swooped down on the schoolyard,
where he took us by surprise.

He leapt across the blacktop
in a single bounding stride,
erupting flames and lava
to incinerate the slide.

He reared his huge and scaly head
and flapped his leathery wings,
then set the soccer field ablaze
and blackened all the swings.

56

He cauterized the asphalt
with a sudden, fiery flash.
Then reeled upon the seesaw
and converted it to ash.

He melted all the monkey bars.
The sand was molten glass.
With nothing left to liquefy
he headed for our class.

I doubt we'll soon be rid of him
despite the fires he's set.
You see, our teacher likes him,
so he's now the teacher's pet.

I Finished My Homework

I finished my homework.
It took me all night.
I tried to make sure
I got everything right.

I read every chapter
the teacher assigned.
My eyes grew so bleary
I nearly went blind.

I studied each problem
until my eyes burned.
Researched each detail,
leaving no stone unturned.

I finished my reading
and got out my pen
and pulled up a chair
at my desk in the den.

I answered each question.
I checked every one.
I wrote out my essays.
At last I was done.

By eight in the morning
I'd run out of fuel.
I packed up my backpack
and headed to school.

I handed the teacher
my homework, and then
I noticed, in horror,
I'd used the wrong pen.

The teacher looked puzzled.
I felt my heart sink.
I'd used my trick pen
with invisible ink.

Homework, I Love You

Homework, I love you. I think that you're great.
It's wonderful fun when you keep me up late.
I think you're the best when I'm totally stressed,
preparing and cramming all night for a test.

Homework, I love you. What more can I say?
I love to do hundreds of problems each day.
You boggle my mind and you make me go blind,
but still I'm ecstatic that you were assigned.

Homework, I love you. I tell you, it's true.
There's nothing more fun or exciting to do.
You're never a chore, for it's you I adore.
I wish that our teacher would hand you out more.

Homework, I love you. You thrill me inside.
I'm filled with emotions. I'm fit to be tied.
I cannot complain when you frazzle my brain.
Of course, that's because I'm completely insane. **59**

My Computer Ate My Homework

My computer ate my homework.
Yes, it's troublesome but true,
though it didn't gnaw or nibble
and it didn't chomp or chew.

I was panicked and perplexed
when it consumed my homework whole
as I pressed the Shift and Enter keys
instead of Shift+Control.

It devoured my hours of typing,
every picture, chart, and graph,
and it left me most unsettled
when I thought I heard it laugh.

I would guess it was a virus,
or it could have been a worm,
that deleted every bit
but didn't prompt me to confirm.

I suppose I might have pressed Escape
instead of pressing Save,
but, regardless, that's the last time
it will ever misbehave.

Yes, I found a good solution,
and I smiled to hear the crash
when I chucked it out the window
and it landed in the trash.

Homework Stew

I cooked my math book in a broth
and stirred it to a steaming froth.
I threw in papers—pencils, too—
to make a pot of homework stew.

I turned the flame up nice and hot
and tossed my binder in the pot.
I sprinkled in my book report
with colored markers by the quart.

Despite its putrid, noxious gas,
I proudly took my stew to class.
And though the smell was so grotesque,
I set it on my teacher's desk.

My teacher said, "You're quite a chef.
But still you're going to get an F.
I didn't ask for 'homework stew,'
I said, 'Tomorrow, *homework's due.*'"

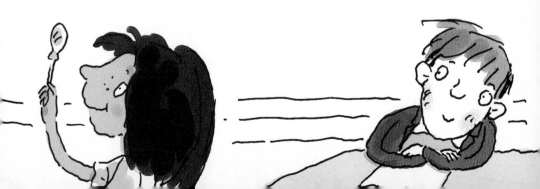

My Dog Does My Homework

My dog does my homework
at home every night.
He answers each question
and gets them all right.

There's only one problem
with homework by Rover.
I can't turn in work
that's been slobbered all over.

December Substitute

Our substitute is strange because
he looks a lot like Santa Claus.
In fact, the moment he walked in
we thought that he was Santa's twin.

We wouldn't think it quite so weird,
if it were just his snowy beard.
But also he has big black boots
and wears these fuzzy bright red suits.

He's got a rather rounded gut
that's like a bowl of you-know-what.
And when he laughs, it's deep and low
and sounds a lot like "Ho! Ho! Ho!"

He asks us all if we've been good
and sleeping when we know we should.
He talks of reindeers, sleighs, and elves
and tells us to behave ourselves.

And when it's time for us to go
he dashes out into the snow.
But yesterday we figured out
just what our sub is all about.

We know just why he leaves so quick,
and why he's dressed like Old Saint Nick
in hat and coat and boots and all:
He's working evenings at the mall.

66

World's Hardest Test

Preparing today for the standardized test
our teacher said there was a lot to digest.
We'd have to divide by the square root of three
and learn to spell *zygote*, *façade*, and *marquis*.

We'd need to play xylophone, trumpet, and flute,
accordion, banjo, piano, and lute;
recite all the capital cities by heart;
and learn to take rocket ship engines apart.

We'd have to speak Latin, Swahili, and Greek;
learn nuclear fusion and fencing technique;
remember the fables of Persia and Rome;
and crack all the codes in the human genome.

Then just when we thought that our heads might explode
from learning Chinese or dissecting a toad,
she told us the very best thing she could say,
that she was just kidding; it's April Fools' Day.

69

It's Friday the Thirteenth Tomorrow

It's Friday the thirteenth tomorrow.
A black cat just leapt in my path.
I'm not superstitious, but this might
explain why I'm failing in math.

By chance I walked under a ladder
a teacher had placed near the wall.
In class my umbrella popped open,
and that's why I tripped in the hall.

The salt spilled this morning at breakfast.
While walking I stepped on a crack.
I set down my shoes on the table.
It looks like my future is black.

This evening I busted a mirror,
which means that the next seven years
are due to be filled with misfortune,
catastrophes, mishaps, and tears.

With all the bad luck I'm confronting,
it seems that I'm probably cursed.
It may be the thirteenth tomorrow,
but Thursday the twelfth is the worst.

THURS
12

71

Halloween Party

We're having a Halloween party at school.
I'm dressed up like Dracula. Man, I look cool!
I dyed my hair black, and I cut off my bangs.
I'm wearing a cape and some fake plastic fangs.

I put on some makeup to paint my face white,
like creatures that only come out in the night.
My fingernails, too, are all pointed and red.
I look like I'm recently back from the dead.

My mom drops me off, and I run into school
and suddenly feel like the world's biggest fool.
The other kids stare like I'm some kind of freak—
the Halloween party is not till next week.

Index

Also from Meadowbrook Press

The Aliens Have Landed at Our School!

Author Kenn Nesbitt, a brilliant new star in the poetry galaxy, writes with the rhythmic genius of Jack Prelutsky and the humor of Bruce Lansky. Children will love the imaginative world of Kenn Nesbitt, a world with mashed potatoes on the ceiling, skunks falling in love, antigravity machines, and aliens invading the school—all wonderfully brought to life in illustrations by Margeaux Lucas.

If Kids Ruled the School

Guaranteed to make you giggle, grin, and guffaw, this anthology is brimming with side-splitting poetry from Bruce Lansky, Kenn Nesbitt, and others. It touches on subjects like homework, tests and grades, show-and-tell, falling asleep in class, school lunches, awkward moments, bad hair, and the ups and downs experienced by every student in school.

No More Homework! No More Tests!

A hilarious collection of poems about school by the most popular children's poets, including Shel Silverstein, Jack Prelutsky, Bruce Lansky, Kenn Nesbitt, David L. Harrison, Colin McNaughton, Kalli Dakos, and others who know how to find humor in any subject.

Rolling in the Aisles

Selected by Bruce Lansky, *Rolling in the Aisles* is Lansky's fourth hardcover anthology of humorous poems for children. It contains funny poems selected by a panel of more than 1,000 elementary-school students. Shel Silverstein, Jack Prelutsky, Bruce Lansky, Kenn Nesbitt, Ted Scheu, Robert Pottle, and Dave Crawley all made the cut for this giggle-packed collection of rhymes.

Kids Pick the Funniest Poems

Three hundred elementary-school kids will tell you that this book contains the funniest poems for kids—because they picked them! Not surprisingly, they chose many of the funniest poems ever written by favorites like Shel Silverstein, Jack Prelutsky, Jeff Moss, Judith Viorst, Bruce Lansky, and Kenn Nesbitt (plus poems by lesser-known writers that are just as funny). This book is guaranteed to please children ages 6–12!

A Bad Case of the Giggles

Be prepared to hear chuckles, chortles, hoots, and hollers when kids discover this anthology of funny poems from Bruce Lansky, Kenn Nesbitt, and others. It will leave them with "a bad case of the giggles."

Miles of Smiles

The third book in Bruce Lansky's highly successful series of humorous children's poetry anthologies. It features poets" like Bruce Lansky, Kenn Nesbitt, Robert Pottle, Ted Scheu, and more.

For more poetry fun, check out
…epoetry.com and **www.poetry4kids.com!**

…titles written to delight, inform, and entertain.
…browse our full selection of titles, visit our website at:

75

…dowbrookpress.com

…an order, request a free catalog, or ask a question:

1-800-338-2232

…ss • 5451 Smetana Drive • Minnetonka, MN • 55343